# COMBAT AIR PATROL

'The heat is on'

# COMBAT AIR PATROL

# IAN BLACK

**Airlife**

# ACKNOWLEDGEMENTS

Many people have helped in the making of this book. The list of friends and fighter pilots is large: Mork, Gibbon, Doof, Archie, Don, Ricko, Bob, Woody, Buckett and CT from the RAF; Keith Hatley, Mike Beachy Head and Ralph Garlick from Thunder City; Grata, Nayot, Nanar, Salva and friends from the French Air Force; and other fighter pilots from the USAF, RDAF, RNoAF and Spain. Thanks!

A big thank you to Fuji UK – not only for supplying Velvia, the best slide film for serious photographers, but also their continued support. To those I've forgotten – the cheque's in the post!

The author in the cockpit of his Mirage 2000C fighter

Copyright © 2003 Ian Black

First published in the UK in 2003
by Airlife Publishing Ltd

**British Library Cataloguing-in-Publication Data**
A catalogue record for this book
is available from the British Library

ISBN 1 84037 336 9

Printed in China

*Contact us for a free catalogue that describes the complete range of Airlife books for pilots and aviation enthusiasts.*

# Airlife Publishing Ltd
101 Longden Road, Shrewsbury, SY3 9EB, England
E-mail: sales@airlifebooks.com
Website: www.airlifebooks.com

# FOREWORD

When those brave pilots of the 1914–18 war duelled over the skies of France few would have believed what the future held for aerial warfare. By the mid-1920s the last of the biplanes were in service, soon to be replaced with metal monoplanes capable of speeds in excess of 400 mph. The Second World War saw the development of the jet engine and unmanned rocket fighters. The result of this frenzied period of development came to fruition in the 1950s. Speed and altitude records were being broken almost on a daily basis, and new and radical wing shapes were being flown on prototypes around the world. Like those who went before them, test pilots in this era were the bravest of the brave, pushing the boundaries of technology and design. By the mid-1950s pilots had broken the sound barrier and then amazingly exceeded the 1,000 mph milestone. In forty years aviation had progressed from the Sopwith Camel, cruising at under 100 mph, to the Fairey Delta 2 at 1,000 mph. One wonders what we would be flying now had the pace of development continued beyond the first thirty years of aviation.

This book is not intended to be a comprehensive coverage of types or eras. It is simply a collection of images of jet fighters from the early era (Meteor) to the present day (F-16). Despite my comments above about the rate of progress, one only has to look at the Meteor, with its thirsty engines and quirky handling, to the third generation of fighters today. The F-16, Tornado and Mirage 2000 are products of development. Fly-by-wire, head-up displays, digital engine-control systems, multi-mode radars and on-board sensors, all these improvements have been the result of continuous development. From the early F-86s to the F-4 Phantom was a huge leap in capability. After the F-4 came the F-15 and F-16 – again a huge leap foreword. The major aerial conflicts of the past fifty years have also shaped the design of the modern jet fighter. The Korean War came soon after the end of the second World War and saw the Hawker Sea Fury pitted against the first-generation MiG-15 jets. By the time of the Vietnam War the F-4 was entering service with its awesome weapon capability, although it took several years to mature into an all-aspect radar-missile-equipped fighter. The Vietnam era saw classic fighters earn their wings – the F-100, F-105, F-4 and F-8 Crusader, to name but a few. The Israeli Six-Day War saw the MiG-21 and Mirage III second-generation fighters cut their teeth.

The Cold War period saw the former Soviet Union produce some classic fighters. The MiG-21, MiG-23 and Su-22 were produced in huge numbers. On the other side of the fence the Royal Air Force continued alone with the VSTOL (vertical or short take-off and landing) concept until the US Marines also introduced the Harrier. Once again it's hard to imagine that the P.1127 (Harrier prototype) first flew just forty years after the end of World War I. The concept of VSTOL operations has taken nearly fifty years to perfect: the JSF (Joint Strike Fighter) will enter service later this decade. By the late seventies the third-generation fighters were hitting the streets. The F-16 set the benchmark standard for lightweight multi-role fighters. Europe produced the Tornado, a multi-role combat aircraft that had its own dedicated Air Defence version. Meanwhile France produced the Mirage 2000, similar in appearance to its predecessor, the Mirage III, but a totally new aircraft. In the Soviet Union fuzzy satellite images of their third-generation fighters began to appear. The MiG-29 bore a striking resemblance to the F-18, and the Su-27 was more than similar to the F-15. These third-generation machines enthralled air show spectators with their manoeuvrability and agility at all speeds.

By the early 1980s the Cold War was coming to an end, but development of fourth-generation fighters was already under way. So far the Saab Grippen is the only fourth-generation fighter to see service in any numbers. The Dassault Rafale has begun limited introduction with the *Aéronavale*, while in Europe the Eurofighter programme is beginning to come to fruition. Across 'the Pond' it will still be some time before the F-22 Raptor and F-35 JSF are on line.

The images in this book are therefore a tribute to the flamboyant jet period 1950–2000, an era when men and machines were still exploring new boundaries – pushing the envelope.

**Tornado Formation.** Tornado F-3s from No. 11 Squadron hold tight formation over their native Yorkshire scenery. The two black eagles have been on the squadron tails since the early 1930s. The two eagles symbolise the squadron's two-seat aircraft, although for many years it operated the single-seat Lightning fighter. Unlike modern fighters, the Air Defence Tornado is a pure interceptor and is unable to perform air-to-ground missions. This makes the aircraft quite limited in a war scenario.

ABOVE:

**Team Work.** A Mirage 2000C takes on fuel from an American-built KC-135 tanker. Operated by the *Armée de l' Air*, the KC-135 is known in France as the C-135FR – C for Cargo, F for French and R for Re-engined, after the fleet was re-engined in 1985 with the CFM56-2. Operated by the 93rd Squadron, 'Bretagne', the French 135s will be in service for many years to come.

**Aerobatic Tornado.** In an aircraft specially painted for the aerobatic season, pilot Archie Niell looks for a cloud break to let down to low level.

7

**Multi-Role Mirage.** Reworked Air Defence Mirage F1 No. 271 is capable of performing both air-to-air and air-to-ground missions.

BELOW:
**Classic Phantom**, before the fitting of the fin-mounted radar-warning receiver. Even by the mid-1980s this particular F-4 seems to have been hard used.

Low-altitude intercepts are some of the most exciting flying a fighter crew can perform. Flying low to the ground, taking part in multi-aircraft engagements is an acquired skill. This Tornado F-3 of No. 23 Squadron has its wings swept at 45 degrees, optimizing the aircraft's speed and turn performance.

**Sunset.** Air Defence crews are used to flying day and night combat air patrols. The silhouette emphasises the clean lines of the Air Defence version of the Tornado.

**Mirage Tails.** In the 1950s rows of fighter aircraft were a common sight throughout Europe and the United States. By the mid-1970s hardened aircraft shelters were becoming highly fashionable and aircraft disappeared from view. Taken at *l'Armée de l'Air* Base *Orange* deep in Provence, the picture captures all three of the wing's squadrons – E/C 1/5, E/C 2/5 and E/C 3/5. The 3/5 has since been disbanded.

**The Last Crusade.** Long after the US Navy retired the F-8 Crusader, the French *Aéronavale* soldiered on with this classic fighter, a veteran of the Vietnam War. The jump in technology from the F-8 Crusader to the Rafale has been staggering. In order to keep their ageing fleet airworthy the French upgraded the aircraft several times. They also bought several ex-US Navy airframes to use as spares.

**A Day in Provence.** A six-ship of Mirage 2000s flies low over the beautiful French countryside.

OPPOSITE:
**Going UP.** Archie Niell puts the display Tornado into a vertical climb.

ABOVE:
Mission accomplished, a two-seat Lightning trainer bearing the markings of the Lightning Training Flight comes to a halt. It is a classic British winter scene. Easily apparent are the extremely-high-pressure thin tyres, designed to fit snugly into the wing.

BELOW:
**Old and New.** A newly delivered F-16A of the Belgian Air Force sits on our wing as an RAF Phantom pulls alongside. The arrival of the F-16 was the first signal that the reign of supremacy the FGR2 had enjoyed for many years was over. At this stage the F-16s were delivered with the original-style black radome.

OPPOSITE:
**Warplane Extraordinaire.** Without doubt the Mirage 2000 is one of the most agile fighter aircraft in service anywhere in the world: the ultimate boys' toy!

**Pre-Flight.** Bob Bees, an RAF exchange pilot, runs through his pre-flight checks prior to a 1 vs 1 air combat mission. For many years pilots from the USAF have flown RAF aircraft and RAF pilots have flown with the USAF.

BELOW:
**Clean Wing.** The F-4 Phantom was a capable dogfighter. This red-tailed FGR2 belongs to No. 56 Squadron, 'The Firebirds' and is flown by Flt Lt Rick Offord.

The F-18 has developed into one of the world's most capable third-generation combat fighters. With its twin-engined reliability and rugged airframe it is more than equal to the F-16 Fighting Falcon.

Returning to base, an RAF Tornado and a Danish Air Force F-16 Falcon. Having just participated in a major NATO exercise in the Baltic, the pair were captured at height prior to landing at Skydstrup Air Base. The F-16, overshadowed by the Tornado, is destined to be the classic fighter pilot's aircraft. Small and highly manoeuvrable, it is what every fighter pilot dreams of.

By its very nature the fighter pilot's job
carries fairly high risks. Luckily most
air forces look after their valuable pilots
should they get into trouble. Seen here
is a Wessex helicopter of No. 84
Squadron rescuing a downed pilot.
Search and rescue pilots are the unsung
heroes of any conflict, putting their lives
at risk to recover downed airmen.

Armed and ready, a *l'Armée de l'Air* pilot runs through his pre-take-off checks prior to a combat air patrol over Bosnia. Based at Cervia on the Italian coast, he will be airborne for four or five hours droning over the sky. He may be called upon to fulfil a variety of tasks, from air-to-air combat to air-to-ground attacks, the hardest job of all being close air support. Co-ordinating with a ground controller, the workload in a single-seat cockpit is extremely high. Trying to find a needle in a haystack is a good analogy for the job of looking for a tank in a wood several miles away. All this while flying your fighter at 400+ mph. In modern warfare avoiding civilian casualties is always at the front of any pilot's mind.

Hawker Hunters had been withdrawn from front-line service many years before this photo was taken in 1992. Operated by the Lossiemouth Buccaneer squadrons, the two-seat Hunters were used to train RAF Buccaneer pilots, of which there was no dual-control version. Painted to represent the famous Black Arrows (although not in gloss paint), most of the Hunters were preserved when they were retired in the early 1990s.

ABOVE:
Ian Wood, now a Tornado squadron commander, dodges the clouds in his Hawk T1a armed with an ACMI pod. Because of its size and excellent handling qualities the Hawk is a difficult adversary.

LEFT:
Tomcats, Hornets and Mirages during Operation *Deny Flight* over the Adriatic in 1996.

Cruising at altitude because of poor low-level weather, this *l'Armée de l'Air* Jaguar is one of a dying breed of NATO fighters. It is one of the few fighters in service that is devoid of an inertial navigation attack system. Using just a map, stopwatch and GPS, the pilots produce remarkable work. The French Jaguar will be the first type to be replaced by the Dassault Rafale.

High over northern Italy, an E/C 2/5 Mirage 2000 pilot holds formation on the camera ship. Taken after a diversion to Istrana Air Base, the aircraft is in the light combat fit, armed with heat-seeking missiles only.

BELOW:
Bristling with weapons is a USAFE F-4G Wild Weasel Phantom. Engines running, the crew await taxi clearance from an overseas visit to RAF Finningley, in Yorkshire. The base has since closed. Operational till the end, the F-4Gs were last in action during the Gulf War.

Every fighter pilot has to start somewhere. The clean lines of the Jet Provost, the basic trainer of the RAF for many years, are evident in this line astern view. Carrying no weapons or weapon-aiming devices, the Jet Provost's role was to teach pure flying skills.

BELOW:
**Eagle Driver.** With another F-15 reflected in his visor, this USAF pilot sits with canopy open prior to a Gulf War mission from Dhahran Air Base. Having removed all the identity patches from his flying suit, this Eagle driver is obviously prepared for the worst. During the war no F-15Cs were lost to enemy action, although a couple of F-15Es were written off.

**9 G Break.** The F-16 was the first jet fighter stressed to pull 9 G on a regular basis (other fighters could pull 9 G but would spend weeks in the hangar afterwards!). The 9 G limit is about the maximum that a fighter pilot can realistically stand without blacking out. Tolerance to G is a combination of many factors – pilot size, weight, fitness, etc. The Israeli Air Force make a point of flying their aircraft to their structural limit on every mission, and this gave them the edge in aerial conflicts during the sixties and seventies.

**ABOVE:**
This 1960s-vintage Lightning bears none of the modern aerodynamic stealth features of modern fighters. Angular and slab-sided, the Lightning achieved most of its prowess through sheer brute force . . . THRUST. This example, flown by Marc Ims, is now preserved in an air museum.

**BELOW:**
Mirage 2000Cs 55 and 56 await their pilots prior to a massive 8 vs. 16 mission on the UK North Sea ACMI range. The *l'Armée de l'Air* has a high operational readiness capability, most of its fighters flying with a fully loaded gun on every mission. This philosophy has become particularly relevant after the events of 11 September 2001. Air forces now have the ability to vector fighters on training missions to interrogate any aircraft over their territory should the need arise.

**Tornado Tails.** After four hard weeks of air-to-air gunnery, these No. 25 Squadron fighters are fitted with long-range ferry tanks prior to the long haul home. Cyprus to UK is around five hours' flying time.

**Desert Storm.** During the Gulf Conflict the *l'Armée de l'Air* deployed a sizeable force to General Chuck Horner's Coalition forces. On the jet combat side, Mirage 2000s, Mirage F1s and Jaguars were deployed to Al Hasa, south of Dhahran. Although they were a welcome asset, one problem was 'like types': the Iraqi Air Force also operated the Mirage F1, which could have caused confusion to Allied pilots. Here, ground crew pre-flight a 5th Wing Mirage 2000C.

**Night Attack.** A Mirage 2000B trainer plugs in the burners in search of its prey.

Tornado F-3s from Nos 11, 25 and 29
(since disbanded) Squadrons take on
fuel from a Victor tanker high over the
Nevada desert. The charismatic Victor
was operational right to the end of its
service life, supporting fighters around
the globe. Starting off as a strategic
bomber, the Victor was employed in the
roles of tanker, bomber and long-range
reconnaissance aircraft.

Insect-like, the Harrier T4 would never win prizes for being a handsome aircraft. Resembling a praying mantis in shape, the T4 is now pretty much a thing of the past, replaced by the modern T10. The RAF donated most of the surplus trainers to the Royal Navy's Fleet Air Arm.

BELOW:
**Last of the Gunfighters.** When I took this photograph in 1997 the F-8 was nearly forty years old. Armed with a gun and Magic 2 infra-red missile, it was hopelessly outclassed by the end of the Millennium. Despite its antiquity, the pilots who flew these charismatic fighters were an elite band, keeping alive a legend from the Vietnam era.

With a last check that his canopy is clear, a USAF F-4G pilot looks skyward for inspiration. About to perform a 2 vs 2 air combat mission against RAF FGR2s, the USAF crews are obviously keen to maintain national pride.

Few, if any, modern-day fighters are as beautiful as the Marcel Dassault Mirage 2000. Armed with a centre-line fuel tank, this machine is from E/C 2/5 based at Orange Air Base. Originally the 2/5 was formed in England and had No. 340 Squadron Free French Air Force allocated. The unit is now the operational conversion unit for the Mirage 2000.

**Lightning Pilot.** Ian Hollingworth occupies the instructor's seat of a twin-seat trainer while a single-seater sits close by. Every air force has its elite fleet, and the Lightning was for many years the RAF's. Single-seated and complex to operate, it was every fighter pilot's dream.

ABOVE:

**War Mission.** A Mirage 2000C armed with live Magic 2 missiles watches closely as an Italian Air Force Tornado bomber takes on fuel. For some reason the Italian Air Force calls the Tornado PA200 – a throwback from the early days when the aircraft was known as the Panavia 200. The fuel venting from the fin of the Tornado indicates its tanks are full and the refuel is nearly complete. Taking fuel from the French-style tanker is a tricky operation, pilots preferring the wing-mounted basket and drogue method used by many air forces.

**In the Beginning.** The Gloster Meteor is still in service in 2002, some fifty years after it was introduced as the RAF's first jet fighter. This example (WH453), conspicuously painted, belongs to the Ministry of Defence at Llanbedr Airfield in Wales. Used as either a shepherd aircraft or airborne target, the Meteor has resisted attempts to replace it by the Hawk or Alpha Jet trainers.

**Mission Accomplished.** After a flight the pilot of this No. 11 Squadron Tornado extends his flight-refuelling probe. This gives ground crews a chance to check for any damage caused by the tanker. Unlike the bomber version, the Tornado ADV (Air Defence Variant) has the retractable probe flush mounted.

RESCUE

ABOVE:
The Mirage 2000D is similar in many respects to the Mirage 2000B Air Defence Variant. With its air-to-ground radar, the twin-seater is rarely seen without its large under-wing fuel tanks. This example is seen with the practice bomb dispenser mounted under the fuselage.

**691.** An F-16B of the Royal Norwegian Air Force. Peculiar to the Norwegian F-16s is the brake parachute housed below the fin. Many modern fighters have special coatings on the canopy to reflect laser energy, used to blind pilots.

**Phantoms.** A well-worn XV400 of No. 19 (Fighter) Squadron joins the grey-green XV439 for the break at the Italian Air Force Base at 'Deci' (Decimomannu). Flown clean, except for Sidewinder pylons, the FGR2 was a potent adversary below 20,000 feet. With its Rolls-Royce Spey engines optimised for low-altitude operations, it was no performer at height however.

Captain Johnny 'C', a French Air Force pilot, coasts in over the Italian Riviera after a combat air patrol over Bosnia. Armed with long-range tanks and Mk 82 iron bombs, the Mirage has just spent the last five hours over enemy territory. Undertaking a CAS (Close Air Support) mission, its pilot, a seasoned campaigner, has flown both in the Gulf Conflict and in Bosnia.

**Beautiful Lightning.** XP693, the company mount of British Aerospace for many years, taxies past the Binbrook line. Once the flagship of the company base at Warton, Lancashire, it is now in private hands. Initially it was retired to Exeter for possible use in the UK. When that deal fell through it was moved to Thunder City in Capetown. As of September 2002 the aircraft was still grounded. One of Thunder City's more ambitious plans is to rebuild the aircraft with a new two-seat nose. Obviously, on the civilian market a dual-control aircraft is more useful than a single-seater.

Wearing his desert flying-suit, an *Armée de l'Air* Mirage pilot comes up close to the photo ship. Armed with the Matra Super 530 missile, the Mirage is more than a match for any NATO adversary.

The super-sleek Mirage F1 never achieved the same success as its predecessor, the Mirage 3. A superb aircraft, it is still in service throughout the world in various guises. This machine is an Air Defence version detached to Corsica from its home base at Rheims.

**Wide-angle F-3**. By today's standards the Tornado Foxhunter radar is massive, compared with modern fighters. After years of upgrades the F-3 is now a viable weapon system.

**Blackbird, Kelly Johnson's SR-71.** Few aircraft have looked as sinister as the Blackbird. Photographed over Mildenhall, England, the Blackbird was once a regular sight in eastern England.

Another Blackbird: Thunder City's Black Arrow Hunter F6, a living legend. Once operated by No. 111 Squadron, this particular aircraft was Number 2 in a 22-aircraft loop at the Farnborough air show. Apart from the Shell logo, the aircraft is as it was almost fifty years ago.

ABOVE:
**Arctic Mirage.**

RIGHT:
**Mirage IV.** With its single-seat-style cockpit and two-man-crew, the Mirage IV is a monster of a jet. Originally designed as France's *force de frappe* aircraft, it has had a long and distinguished career. Now relegated to reconnaissance duties, the Mirage IV has always been cloaked in a veil of secrecy, largely because of its nuclear role. A little known fact is that the RAF looked at buying the Dassault bomber during the period of the TSR2 and F-111, when it would naturally have been fitted with Rolls-Royce powerplants.

OPPOSITE:
Mirage 2000 No. 56, armed with Mk 82 500 lb bombs on the shoulder pylons, awaits its pilot.

44

ABOVE:
The original Hawker Harrier GR3. This bug-like fighter was not the easiest aircraft to fly, and the RAF's accident rate was extremely high. Seen here is a machine belonging to No. 3 Squadron, one of the RAF's oldest squadrons and a long-time Harrier operator.

'Black Bucc' Mike Beachy Head roars over the South African crowd in his personal Buccaneer. The wings, shrouded in mist, show just how hard he's pulling.

**Combined Forces Operations.** Fighter pilots get some pretty amazing views of the world. As my wingman and I joined this US KC-10 tanker we were joined by a gaggle of US Navy F-18s.

ABOVE:
Ultra-clean, a Mirage 2000 of E/C 1/5 turns finals at Orange Air Base. Just above the canopy is the single north–south runway.

RIGHT:
Almost like a brass rubbing, the low setting sun accentuates the lines of this RAF Lightning T5. This particular machine, XV328, was the penultimate Lightning built for the RAF. Today only the nose-section survives.

OPPOSITE:
A lesson I learnt from a legendary aviation photographer was to find the clouds and then position the aircraft around them. Taking his advice I placed these three Lightnings into the sun during a low winter sunset.

The image many of the early jet pilots must have seen, line astern in a Meteor F.8. The Meteor was sold to many countries, from Argentina to Australia.

Early Harrier GR5s from both the OCU and No. 1(F) Squadron break away from the camera. Since this picture was taken, all the RAF's Harriers have been upgraded to GR7 standard.

A classic image of the legendary F-16. Most fighter aircraft achieve legendary status after they have been withdrawn from service. The F-16 Fighting Falcon can truly lay claim to the fame of being legendary. In service throughout the world, it is unquestionably one of the world's greatest fighters ever made. What it lacks in range it more than makes up for in punch. This F-16 from the Belgian Air Force has since been upgraded to near F-16C standard.

BELOW:
An Anglo/French Jaguar fighter of the 1970s awaits its tanker slot. Flown clean it's a relatively agile fighter in experienced hands.

**Armed and Dangerous.** Everything out for the camera, a clean Tornado F-3 prepares to fly a training mission just prior to the Gulf War. In an effort to reduce workload the aircraft were flown with live weapons during both training and war missions.

ABOVE:
From any angle the F-104 Starfighter is a beautiful fighter. This is an early-1980s shot of an Italian F-104 on our Phantom's wing.

BELOW:
No. 23 Squadron was the fourth RAF squadron to receive the Tornado F-3. Having previously operated the Phantom and Lightning, it became the first Tornado unit to disband. The unit now operates E3 Sentry aircraft at RAF Waddington.

**Eagle Driver.** A very English pilot in his very American office – the F-15 Eagle.

Lightning squadrons had a long association with painted tails. Starting in the 1960s with No. 74 Squadron 'Tigers', the tradition carried on to the end with No. 11 Squadron's black-finned XR725.

An unusual mixed formation led by a
Harrier T4 and a pair of Hunter T7s
(painted in Black Arrow colours). A lone
Phantom from No. 56 Squadron adds to
the colour.

Gear down, the Meteor U16 (U for 'Unmanned') turns finals for Llanbedr Airfield on the Welsh coast. This sparsely populated area is ideal for unmanned jet operations.

BELOW:
**Dirty Bucc.** Long after the Gulf War aircraft returned to the UK, their hastily applied desert schemes were a common sight. This Buccaneer diverted into RAF Leeming some months after the war was over. General wear and tear and copious hydraulic and oil leaks have added to its used look.

Tanking from a C-130 is not as easy as it
looks  as with its relatively slow speed
(in fighter terms),  it leaves little margin
for error. As the fighter takes on more
fuel it becomes heavier, making contact
harder. Occasionally a technique known
as 'tobogganing' is employed, where
the tanker starts a slow descent to keep
its speed up.

Tiger Starfighter pilot, RAF Brawdy,
1992.

XR773, once an RAF Lightning, now privately owned, pictured in August 2002 against a table-top background. The F-6 Lightning, once the pride of 11 (F) Squadron, is now the pride of Thunder City.

Armed with a centre-line fuel tank and two wing tanks, the FGR2 had an impressive range. Used in this fit for QRA (quick reaction alert) and ferry missions, the three-tank fit was a common sight in the UK.

RIGHT:
Popping flares, Ian McDonald Webb checks his flare system is working prior to a *Desert Shield* sortie.

OPPOSITE:
Mirage F1C No. 87. A few of the *Armée de l' Air* Mirages were painted in desert schemes for use in Northern Africa.

From certain angles the Tornado F-3 looks every inch a fighter. Its greatest asset is its unmatched low-level acceleration and top speed. The pilot is Mark Graham – a long-time fighter pilot – here flying over the north Yorkshire countryside.

The back-seat view from a Hawk of a remotely controlled Jindivik unmanned target. Similar in size to the Jet Provost and powered by the same Viper engine, the 'Jindy' has been around for many years. Whenever the unmanned Jindy is launched a chase aircraft is always airborne.

A Mirage 2000C of the now defunct
E/C 3/5.

**Red Flag 1992.** The ground crew give this Tornado F-3 a last-chance check. Planning and leading a Red Flag mission is one of the highlights of any fighter pilot's career. Red Flag is about as close as you get to combat without being shot down!

ABOVE:
Always one of my favourite aircraft, the F-8 Crusader was a true fighter pilot's aircraft. Single-engined, agile for its day and multi-role capable, the Crusader earned the respect of a generation of pilots during the Vietnam War.

BELOW:
The Cold War, RAF Phantoms and RAF Germany are all now a distant memory.

For many years the RAF F-4s ruled the skies over central Europe. With their Westinghouse AWG12 radar and awesome firepower, the RAF Phantoms were highly respected NATO players.

Holding a tight echelon, Jake Jarron, then OC No. 11 Squadron, flies the wing flagship XR728 JS.

After four solid weeks of air-to-air
gunnery this Tornado F-3 of No. 25
Squadron looks decidedly dirty.

The hardest part of photographing nine aircraft together is trying to put air between each airframe to achieve a balanced look. No. 56 Squadron do the camera proud with this diamond nine of Phantoms.

In the early 1990s the unthinkable happened and Warsaw Pact fighters began flying in UK airspace. Russian MiG-29s arrived at the Farnborough Air Show, followed by the Czech Air Force flying into Fairford. MiG-21s, 23s, 29s and Su-22s and 27s were all common visitors. At last it gave the West the chance to examine the Soviet hardware at close quarters. Some RAF pilots were also lucky enough to fly back-seat in the MiGs and Sukhois. Here a MiG-29 formates on an RAF Hawk trainer.

Plan form Phantom. With its upturned wings and down-turned stabilator it was unlike any other fighter of its day.

ABOVE:
August 1990 was a tense time for RAF pilots. Having trained for years against a threat from the East they were suddenly faced with a very different enemy. Tornado F-3s were hurriedly brought up to specification and deployed to the Gulf for combat air patrol duties.

When we had finished our 4 vs 4 DACT (dissimilar air combat training) mission, the Crusaders took the lead and escorted us back to their home base on the north-west tip of France. The lead F-8 pilot kept the speed high at Mach 0.9+ as we started to descend. The cloud and light looked perfect for this atmospheric picture.

**Nine from 56.** High over the North Sea nine Phantoms fly the classic diamond nine pattern. Despite it looking inviting, the cold North Sea is anything but. For eight to nine months of the year RAF pilots who fly over the sea wear the full exposure suit essential for survival in the cold water.

As a fighter pilot, air shows leave me cold. The real buzz is watching and taking part in large joint exercises. Participating with other air forces and mixing with other fighters is what it's all about. Here three Royal Norwegian F-16s taxi out for a mission with six RAF Tornado F-3s during a tactical fighter meet in 1992. The aircraft, operating from Andoya, north of the Arctic Circle, are about to take on a mixed force of Tornado bombers, F-5s and Danish F-16s.

This is just about the exact view a pilot sees when he is in close formation with another Tornado. Holding the same position is all about picking reference points and holding the same picture. On a clear day it can be enormously satisfying to fly close formation. The real aim of the exercise is to penetrate cloud as a single unit day or night or in all weathers. When all you can see is your leader's wingtip it certainly concentrates the mind.

BELOW:
A fresh coat of paint and this RAF FGR2 Phantom looks as good as new. In fact XV470 had already been in service for fifteen years. Having undergone many upgrades by the time this picture was taken, the aircraft carried on in service right to the end of the Phantom force, some ten years later. Al Chubb low-flies the aircraft here over the Belgian countryside.

**Over the top.** The Mirage 2000C has superb low-speed handling qualities. Its big delta wing makes it the ultimate 'turning machine'. As the speed drops and the alpha (angle of attack) builds up, the leading edge slats deploy automatically, giving the wing more lift. This particular aircraft has the underside painted black to celebrate the fiftieth anniversary of 340 Free French Air Force Squadron.

BELOW:
Mirage 2000 family photo: Mirage 2000C, Mirage 2000N and Mirage 2000D. The light grey aircraft is from E/C 1/5. The 'N' version is a nuclear strike aircraft, and the 'D' is pure strike.

**Back-seat F-16.** All fighter pilots jump at the chance of the opportunity to fly other types. Flying back-seat of the F-16 is an awesome experience, the ride at low level superb. In terms of look-out the canopy is excellent and the performance eye-watering. The photo was taken returning from a TASMO (TActical Support of Maritime air Operations) mission deep in the Baltic Sea.

ABOVE:
RAF Phantoms were always dirty, unlike those of the USAF, whose aircraft were kept in pristine condition. The RAF aircraft were more warlike in appearance; in fact all the oil and fluid had an anti-corrosive quality. XV400 (F) of No. 19 Squadron returns from a 1 v 1 combat sortie.

Super-sleek, the Mirage F1B trainer is one of Dassault's most graceful fighters. Seen returning to Mont de Marsan, this example belongs to the l'Armée de l'Air's test and evaluation squadron.

A Mirage F1C in full desert camouflage tows an airborne target back to base. The red-coloured under-fuselage pod holds the drogue, which is released in the air and supported by the two wires from the wingtips. The *l'Armée de l'air* takes air-to-air gunnery very seriously and has some very operational tactics for employing the gun.

Unique in the RAF were the F-4J Phantoms. They were very un-British, lacking the Rolls-Royce Spey engines and Ferranti avionics fitted to true British Phantoms. Nevertheless they were always very tricky opponents. No. 74 Squadron, the sole operators of this variant, normally flew the aircraft clean or centre-line tank only. This example was one of the last 'J's to retain the original US-Navy-style camouflage.

**Falklands Tornado.** The RAF still maintains a force of four Tornado interceptors on the islands. These aircraft come under the title of 1435 Flight, whose claim to fame was the protection of Malta during the Second World War with ancient Gloster Gladiators. As a mark of respect the F-3s are still marked as *Faith*, *Hope* and *Charity*, like the gladiators before them. Should a conflict in the Falklands recur, the islands could be re-enforced at short notice. Don Morrison holds formation as we fly low round the islands.

Known as the 'SEM' in French service, the Super Etendard Modernise is a real workhorse. Similar in shape and size to the Hawker Hunter, it is still a potent warplane despite its age. The Super Etendard is due to be replaced by the Rafale once the Air Defence squadrons are re-equipped.

BELOW:
**Beachy's Bucc.** Thunder City's finest at rest.

Two Mirage 2000s from the Orange wing wait behind the tanker aircraft. The rear aircraft carries an experimental NATO-style grey camouflage, a change from the flamboyant and unique grey/blue normally applied to French fighters.

**Brand-new fully loaded Mirage 2000D.**
The *Armée de l'Air* must take credit for
the way in which it equips its front-line
fighters. Totally indigenous, the *Armée
de l'Air* relies on very little external
foreign support to supply its aircraft.
Extremely talented pilots and
enthusiastic engineers make the French
air force one of the best in the world.

Stray light creates an orange glow around this into-sun shot of Binbrook's finest. Captured mid-turn, John Spencer leads nine Lightning F-6s in an immaculate formation. Streaming wingtip vortices show the G is piling on as the leader tightens the turn.

Chequerboard patterns have long been associated with Air Defence squadrons. No. 19 (F) Squadron are no exception, daubing their aircraft in blue and white checks since the 1930s. XV497 (A) is the squadron commander's aircraft and is liberally coated. On the fin is the stylised Chinese Fighting Dolphin, the squadron's emblem. Raw power at its best: former Lightning jockey John Cliffe tweaks his FGR2 off the hot 'Deci' runway.

ABOVE:
Mark Swan (pilot) and Mick Martin (navigator) lead a formation of Tornado fighters. By tradition No. 25 (F) Squadron is commanded by a navigator with a squadron leader pilot as his deputy.

**Bucc Break.** After the Gulf War I was keen to photograph as many images of 'Gulf' participants as possible, not because I'm an 'anorak', but because I believe passionately in preserving the heritage of the RAF for future generations. Capturing the moment is what it's all about, and here Tim Couston in his Buccaneer breaks from the camera.

ABOVE:
Throughout the 1970s and 1980s airfields across Europe and the Gulf began sprouting hardened aircraft shelters. The once familiar rows of jet fighters disappeared. Re-creating the scene at French Air Force Base Cazaux is a line of sleek Mirage 2000s from both the Cambrai and Orange wings.

BELOW:
**Sleek . . . No . . . Purposeful . . . Yes.** From certain angles the Tornado F-3 looks the part. Tornado driver Ian McDonald Webb runs through his pre-start checks in a No. 23 Squadron Tornado F-3 at RAF Leeming.

**A Dassault Etendard.** Often Air Defence pilots are called upon mid-mission to investigate unknown aircraft as a training exercise. Caught here is this early Etendard of the French Navy cruising at altitude.

When clean the diminutive Hawk can
even give the mighty F-15 a hard time in
a visual combat fight. Of course, with its
magnificent air-to-air radar beyond
visual range, combat against the Eagle is
a different story.

The BAe Hawk has been a huge success around the world. Wearing the markings of No. 151 Squadron, this Hawk came from RAF Chivenor. Both base and squadron have since closed.

'Spanish Hornet' sounds a bit like a love potion, but this EF-18 is a deadly fighter. Painted in standard US Navy colours, the Spanish F-18s form the backbone of their air force.

ABOVE:
From a pilot's point of view there can be few nicer sights than leading a formation of jets for a run in and break. A pair of Mirage 2000s tuck in close, while a third sits low as we head in to French Air Force Solenzara, on the Island of Corsica.

BELOW:
**Fighter Town 'Deci'.** In the late 1970s and 1980s Europe was awash with fighter jets. F-15s, aggressor F-5s and No. 1 Squadron Harriers share the ramp on this Sardinian base. Out of view are RAF F-4s, Italian F-104s and German Phantoms. Also dotted around the base were T-33s, F-100s and G91s acting as airborne targets.

ABOVE:
Tornado silhouette.

Having sat in cloud for fifteen minutes, we finally broke through it a mile from Wildenrath's westerly runway. Close-formation flying in all weathers is bread and butter for fighter pilots.

X5417, a T5 trainer from the Lightning Training Flight, taxies out from the Binbrook line just prior to the end of Lightning operations.

A fighter pilot's office is normally
cramped, and the Mirage F1 is no
exception. With maps crammed down
the coaming, an F1 pilot from Rheims
taxies back to the flight line.

**Brothers in Arms.** A Spanish C-130 tanker gives fuel to two US EA6Bs while a French Mirage looks on. All aircraft are taking part in Operation *Deny Flight* combat air patrols over Bosnia.

A Phantom FGR2 crewed with two pilots awaits start clearance in its revetment. Only a few of the RAF's FGR2s were dual-control versions, used for pilot training.

ABOVE:
A low-angle view of the French Mirage 2000D. Twenty years ago fighters would not have been able to fly with an asymmetric configuration like this. Fly-by-wire technology has changed all this, allowing pilots much greater freedom.

LEFT:
Plan view of a Tornado F-3 from No. 25 Squadron, overflying the River Humber – not the world's prettiest location!

OPPOSITE:
**How close can you get?** Just for my benefit a fellow Mirage 2000 pilot closes up to the lens!

Breaking out, XS904, a Warton-based
Lightning, peels away from the photo
ship. Having paid one final visit to RAF
Germany, the Lightning was returning
to its Lancashire base.

Having spent thirty minutes over a choppy Mediterranean sea chasing Jaguar bombers, our wingmen (a pair of French Navy Crusaders) offer to take us for a fly-by of their carrier, the *Clemenceau*. As I close up on the F-8's wing I can see the carrier in the distance. I get goose bumps when I think of how tiny the runway was – no bigger than a postage stamp. Navy pilots have my full admiration.

BELOW:
**Sunset Tornado.**

ABOVE:
The Italian Air Force is operator of both the Tornado and the F-104 Starfighter. In the early 1990s Italian pilots took the chance to sample the Tornado F-3 during an exchange at the UK base.

LEFT:
The French Air Force uses Mirage F1s in the tactical reconnaissance role.

OPPOSITE:
A Spanish Hornet rolls over the top.

ABOVE:
Since the end of the Gulf War, F-16s of the USAF have remained in theatre. After a 1 vs 1 combat sortie this F-16C comes alongside my Mirage 2000C. The block 50 F-16 is a fantastic fighter and a match for the Mirage.

**Scottish Eagle.** This F-15A from the New Orleans Air National Guard is a long way from home.

An F-16 of the Royal Danish Air Force. As part of an upgrade programme, Danish, Norwegian, Dutch and Belgian F-16s have all received the mid-life update.

Not long after this picture was taken, a
Mirage 2000N was shot down over
Bosnia. Both the crew survived the
ejection but were not given a hospitable
welcome. At the time of this photo
fighters and bombers flew together,
acting as designator and fighter.

ABOVE:
A Mirage IV fighter-bomber in the shadow of Mt Ventoux.

BELOW:
Another famous Tornado unit, No. 5 Squadron, is also a victim of defence cuts.

Originally the unit's aircraft wore red fin bands and fighter-style arrowheads.

Fish-eye view of the Llanbedr hangar.
Among the aged types are Meteors,
Canberras and Sea Vixens

**Sport of Kings.** Flying combat air patrol
in a high-tech fighter is about as good as
it gets.

A clean-wing F-16C returns to its Dhahran base.

**Sleek fighters.**

Mission accomplished – the Mirage
2000 flagship of E/C 2/5.

**Eagles' Nest.** F-15 fighters from Langley Air Base were some of the first to deploy to the Gulf during the invasion of Kuwait.

111

A Tornado formation from No. 20
Squadron over the North York Moors.

# INDEX